THE
AUTISTIC BROTHERS

Two Unconventional Paths to Adulthood

THOMAS CLEMENTS

First pulished in 2018 in England by Thomas Clements

Copyright © 2018 Thomas Clements

This title is available for sale online and from
loads of great bookshops worldwide

Cover design by Phil Clements

Illustrated throughout by Jack Clements

Cover notes by Roy Clements

ISBN: 9781729289389

once upon a time.

1 – INTRODUCTION

I remember the day Jack was born vividly despite being a tiny child at the time. My mum cradled him in her arms as we sat next to one another on the floral settee in our Essex home. I was besotted by the vulnerable little pink-skinned creature I was told repeatedly by my relatives was my brother, a concept of which I'd yet, at that tender age, to grasp the full meaning. There wasn't a hint of jealousy in me over this new addition to the family. In fact, I was more interested at the time in rolling my toy cars over his forehead and dabbing my Polo mints on his lips. The notion of sibling rivalry never even entered my head.

Twenty five years later and things are more or less the same. We're two brothers who've never fought and never been competitive or resentful towards one another in any way. Jack attends a college for people with complex learning disabilities by day while I occupy myself with writing and helping my grandmother. Jack and I are both technically "autistic" and yet represent different experiences of the condition. While Jack is limited verbally, I can speak several languages fluently. Because of his condition, Jack will never be able to live a conventional life. He is unable to work or even to function in day-to-day life. I on the other hand am able to work, but, because of my condition, struggle with social interaction or even the maintenance of friendships. While Jack is happy in his daily routine of going to college, I am almost permanently neurotic and anxious.

Our experiences as brothers have so far been unique, beautiful, at times quite sad, but always interesting. I would love more than anything to share with you our world and to show that there's no rivalry necessary between two autistic brothers.

jack
and thomas

2 – DID HE JUST CALL THAT POLICEMAN A 'WALLY'?

Jack is a lovable person. He's the embodiment of pure innocence and his incredibly open and honest face is testament to this. Never once has Jack coveted anything, envied anyone or spent time worrying over things. Everyone who has come into contact with him is instantly charmed by him, especially given he has a tendency to say things that make people laugh. Jack is 'echolalic' which means that he repeats words and phrases that he's heard either from those around him or from his beloved collection of old films. Although his verbal skills are limited, Jack is often adept at summoning bits of dialogue from films that he watches (his favourite, like many on the spectrum, being Thomas the Tank Engine) and applying those as best he can in the context of ordinary day-to-day dialogue. Despite lacking the ability to form complete sentences and accurate grammar that most neurotypical people can do instinctively, Jack's surprising capacity for remembering large chunks of dialogue he's heard enables him to elicit phrases that he senses fit into the context of what is going on around him. This can be charming, funny and occasionally, highly inappropriate.

My family love to holiday in Italy. For us, it has everything we value in a country. My mother Maria has a special

Peace
man

affinity for the culture and food, so much so that we suspect that she may be a secret Italian herself! Italy's also the ideal place for Jack to go because, unlike in the UK, the people there, being open and animated by nature, are far less conscious of Jack's idiosyncratic behaviours like hand-flapping and talking to himself. Italians are also exceptionally warm towards children and Jack, despite being in an adult's body, will always possess a childlike aura.

Jack's a fussy eater, too, but he's generally always done well in Italy. When he was younger, it was a nightmare to get him to eat things. Autistic people often have peculiar food preferences and stick to a limited diet as a result. One time we were in the city of Naples at a backstreet pizzeria which, I must say, served the most divine pizza I'd ever eaten in my life. While we tucked into pizza alla marinara (the original incarnation of the world famous dish, invented by the wives of Neapolitan fisherman with few ingredients to hand), we were pessimistic Jack would even take a bite out of his. But, to our amazement, he enthusiastically rolled up his sleeves, put a napkin into his collar, grabbed his knife and fork and tackled the gigantic pizza in front of him. He was very thin at the time but he managed about three quarters of this colossal plate of

swimming
PooL

leavened bread and San Marzano tomato. We were so thrilled that we took a photo of him mid-meal that remains in our kitchen to this day. This was infinitely preferable to his usual bland staple of chicken nuggets and chips which he occasionally varies with fish fingers and chips.

Another advantage to Italy is of course its beautiful sunny weather. For Jack, the highlight of his holiday is the swimming pool which is a cool, quiet place where he can bob around on his own for hours on end without concern for the world outside. As children, I was instructed by mum and dad never to mention "swimming pool" before going on holiday because they worried that he might not sleep the night due to sheer excitement. Given the choice, I think Jack would quite happily live in a swimming pool and, on account of his dark, swarthy complexion, would tan beautifully and never suffer sunburn.

Recently I watched a video of him in a pool in Sicily where he appears in a sort of deep autistic trance, flapping his arms excitedly and mumbling entire scripts from Thomas the Tank videos to himself while he wades in idyllic turquoise water. I don't know what it is about Jack, but there's something spellbinding about seeing him in those states. It's not something comprehensible to a neurotypical mind or even a mildly autistic mind like

THomas

mine. I just wish sometimes I could ask him what it is he feels and thinks, how he experiences reality, what he perhaps knows that I don't about the mysteries of the universe. I have so many questions I want to ask him but am sadly unable to.

The best thing about Italy is what Jack is able to get away with without breaking any unwritten laws of social etiquette. This one time, my parents were at a restaurant in the southern state of Calabria, a place slightly off the tourist radar for Brits owing to its reputation as "bandit country" where organised crime syndicates flourish and operate in plain sight. In a place where it might be thought wise to keep a low profile and be as unobtrusive and polite to others as possible, Jack did something that, back home in Britain, might not have gone down too well.

After mum, dad and Jack had finished their meal, Jack did his usual thing of attempting to take the tip left on the table for the waiting staff. We guess he does this because he's anxious we might accidentally leave it behind. Mum, in a light-hearted way said to Jack, "Leave it there, you wally!" (Wally, for any American readers, is a benign and peculiarly British word we use to mean "fool"). Autistic people like Jack are often exacting and have to have things a certain way. When that order is disrupted and things don't fit neatly in their clearly-defined conceptual boxes, like the arbitrary leaving behind of coins on the dining table, Jack tends to get a little agitated. Feeling upset, Jack left the restaurant with the word "wally" repeating itself over and over in his head. As they left the restaurant and were back in whichever town it was they were in, my parents stopped to ask a stern-looking policeman for directions. The proud officer, resplendent in his uniform which was adorned with badges and a string of shiny medals, started speaking in fast and heavily lilted Italian, and Jack, still feeling agitated about leaving the tip, went up close to the policeman, looked directly into his eyes and said, "You wally!" I can only imagine his bemusement. Luckily, he didn't know the meaning of the word and so had no recourse to react to it which, for my terribly embarrassed parents, must have been a huge relief. The incident is now a source of great amusement at family gatherings.

Jack's innocence and blamelessness has the ability to dissolve all of one's petty fears and apprehensions. The things he comes out with are sometimes incredibly rude, but it's just impossible for anyone to feel anger or malice towards him. He lets people see that our little egos that typically lash out are something we should all laugh at from time to time. He puts life into perspective for us as a family which is why I think we're all so close and supportive of one another. He's a great leveller.

3 - THE BOSTON ERA

There was an especially dark period in our family's history upon which I don't particularly like to dwell. It was during the late 90s when a group of parents from all corners of the UK, all with disabled, non-verbal autistic children, got together and campaigned for funding to send their kids to a school in America that purported to be able to "cure" autism using a new Japanese-style discipline regimen. At the time, there was little in the way of support for autistic people and a lot of misinformation flying around about what supposedly caused the condition. Many parents were led to believe by unscrupulous profiteers and conspiracy theorists that their kids had been damaged by vaccines, pharmaceuticals and pollutants in the environment. These parents also felt a righteous sense of indignation at being let down by a government that simply wasn't making adequate provisions for their children. Parents from Scotland to Kent got together and raised enough money through various fundraising events to send their kids to Boston-Higashi. The name is one whose very mention makes Jack shudder. I'm still not entirely sure what went on there, but I know a lot of it wasn't good.

On a wet and cold day in late October, dad and I rushed home from my weekly game of football for the local

Scouts team. I remember being caked in mud from head to toe and absolutely beaming at the thought that I'd soon be up in the clouds en route to a new continent. The fact that this continent was America, source of all popular culture I'd consumed as a kid, was even cooler. The purpose of our trip was to reunite with mum and Jack who'd been at Boston-Higashi for a few months by that time. Landing in Boston was like landing in Siberia.

It was face-searingly cold and the snow was thicker than I'd ever seen before in my life. Big industrial ploughs were needed to keep the runway clear. It was incredible. I remember my dad driving our hire car on the freeway past all the common reference points of American culture like roadside diners, baseball fields, 'Dunkin' Donuts' and big green road signs that read 'Downtown' and 'Interstate'. We arrived in a place just outside Boston City called Randolph at the small apartment where mum was staying. It was about a 10-minute drive from Higashi, where Jack had been boarding up until now.

The relief of being together as a family again was immense, except for one thing: Jack was still at school. He'd been boarding there as part of the school's philosophy which is essentially military-style and authoritarian. The school's method for treating autism consisted of a rigorous exercise and activity schedule, designed with the specific purpose of preventing autistic individuals from retreating into self-absorption as they would do typically if they were left to their own devices. The school's pupils are made to get up early, to keep their living space clean and tidy, to go jogging, to take part in a range of activities that promote 'intellectual stimulation' and to subsist on an austere Japanese diet consisting mainly of rice. It's essentially boot-camp for people with autism, described in the manual euphemistically as a holistic 'Daily Life Therapy'. The reality of this so-called treatment is far less humane, warm and fuzzy as the school's website suggests. There were regular reports of staff abusing students by making them do push-ups as a punishment for bad behaviour, despite many of them having physical disabilities.

It emerged sometime after Jack had left the school that one carer was caught on CCTV pulling the hair of one girl and dragging her across the floor. One pupil at the school was allegedly assaulted by a Japanese staff member who subsequently fled the US to avoid being arrested. Of course at the time, my parents and I had no idea any of this terrible abuse of vulnerable people was going on. Like many parents who'd been abandoned by the state, mine wanted to believe that this place had the answer with its magic method that had received a long list of laudatory reviews.

dirPLane

We went to Higashi the day after arriving in Boston to finally be reunited with Jack whom we hadn't seen for several months. This was the longest time he'd ever been separated from us. The school was having some kind of commemorative event. I can't even remember what the hell it was about, but in any case it required both staff and students to wear traditional Japanese dresses or kimonos. We were all eager to see our beloved Jack whom we'd all fretted over incessantly during his time away from us when we were allowed no contact with him.

Before we were allowed to see him though, he was made to take part in some kind of ceremonial march. It was all pretentious and silly looking back on it. We were standing in the crowd as Jack and his fellow students marched by and we were so desperate to catch a glimpse of him. Hawk-eye that he is, he spotted our faces in a sea of people from quite a distance and broke file from the procession. The look of relief on his face is one I can barely begin to describe and is one that will forever be etched in our memories as a family. He ran straight to his mother who embraced her child with such love it would have melted even the stoniest of hearts. Except of course for those of the Higashi staff, who were horrified by Jack's insubordination and independence of action. One particularly stern Japanese lady insisted he go back and join the march right away. We all refused. This moment was far too special to ruin.

Jack was thin. His arms looked like two twigs and his ribcage was showing. He can't have eaten much there apart from bananas which were the only thing on the menu at Higashi that Jack would agree to eat. It was a bit shocking for us to witness in fact. Jack had always been thin, but he was now beginning to look unhealthy and gaunt. The exercise he had to do every morning had used up every fat supply in his body and what remained really was just skin and bone. He also behaved differently from before. He was speaking a little bit more coherently and, to our amazement, was even able to count. He'd also acquired an American accent while doing so which was quite amusing to us all. One of the phrases he used most was "Can I go to the bathroom?" Whereas before my parents had struggled to toilet-train Jack, he could at least now take himself to the bathroom and clean up after himself. This was one of the major benefits of him living under an authoritarian regime for a while. It forced Jack to do things he wasn't inclined to do but were very necessary in daily life. Another plus point was that Jack was well-liked by staff, albeit purely due to the fact he wasn't as physically disabled as many of the other students who were epileptic and in wheelchairs. This at least saved him

17

from cruel physical abuse, or at any rate we like to think that was the case.

A few months after reuniting with Jack, we withdrew him from Higashi, sensing that while the discipline had done him some good in the long-term, it was basically cruel to continue to subject him to it any longer. Autistic or not, Jack is a human being. He has human needs for love and affection from others, especially his mother. That unique and powerful mother-and-son bond transcended everything and put our lives as a family back into perspective. It was time for Jack to return with us to the United Kingdom where he'd once again feel happy, more secure and return back to a healthy weight again.

4 – OUR SHARED LOVE OF OLD FILMS

Jack is a bit like a recording device. He's able to watch films just a couple of times and memorise entire chunks of dialogue. Throughout much of the day he mutters such dialogue to himself with astonishing accuracy of tone and pronunciation. Why he does this, I don't know but I suspect it serves as a substitute for the way we communicate but minus all the unpredictability. Autistic minds crave certainty and control. This deep, inherent need for patterns, lists and unvarying routines manifests itself in different sorts of behaviours according to the individual. In my case, I get a lot of pleasure from memorising facts, especially those that pertain to my 'special interest' which is human geography. A book of facts, namely an encyclopaedia or atlas, is a therapeutic tool for me. Writing lists of world capitals is something I would do over and over again on lined paper as a way of relieving anxiety and imposing my own certainty on an otherwise chaotic and unfathomable world. Jack does this by reciting lines from old Terry Thomas films, which he adores. He even manages to replicate Thomas's distinctively plummy 1950s accent and in a way that makes everyone smile.

We both enjoy watching these old films together and are able to bond over our shared love of the especially comical, slapstick encounters between Thomas and partner-in-crime, Eric Sykes. One in the film 'Monte Carlo or Bust', perhaps our all-time favourite film of Thomas's entire oeuvre, involves him being shocked with what he calls a "schoolboy buzzer" by cheeky chappy Chester Schofield played by veteran actor Tony Curtis. Jack and I always delight in recreating this scene using all the comical and exaggerated physical gestures whenever we see each other. I greet Jack by shaking his hand to which he invariably begins the famous "schoolboy buzzer" routine. It's really quite comical!

Jack's room is his sanctuary where he feels safe from the uncertainty and chaos of the outside world. It's in this safe space that he can begin the real work of manifesting his true nature and doing exactly what he does best. He'll spend literally hours on end in the same seated position, plugged into his computer watching YouTube clips of Thomas, rewinding them over and over, and then reciting the dialogue to himself until he has fully memorised it. Given the right opportunity in daily life, he'll apply what he has learnt from these film scripts to real life. One such example is when he came back from a college music festival. When he arrived home we asked Jack, "How was the music festival?" to which he replied in Thomas trademark clipped voice "It was a bloody row!" We could not stop laughing.

His bedroom is also kept clean and orderly and anything that shouldn't be there is quickly removed or put back in its correct place. We're both similar in that respect. I too thrive on order and neatness. If my room ever does become messy, it's usually a sign there's something wrong with my mental state. I've frequently lapsed into one of my depressive episodes which effectively stops me from being my true self, which is to say, a person of routine and organisation which some might even deem to be excessive.

It's quite funny that I'm labelled the "high functioning" one in some ways. There are obvious reasons why I am high-functioning compared to Jack. I can perform daily tasks, I can converse, I can go to restaurants on my own, I can cook and I can travel independently. Jack can't do any of these. But the fact is, Jack does not suffer for it.

There isn't any hint of worry or neurosis etched into his face whereas mine has been ravaged by fear, uncertainty and periods of extreme nihilism, mainly due to having to navigate my way through the perils of social interaction and then failing on a very consistent basis. Having to survive at work while frequently misunderstanding co-workers' and bosses' intentions has led me to get

monter

carLo

orBust

things very wrong indeed. I think I've aged pretty quickly due to stress, too. My hair's practically all fallen out, I have deep dark circles under my eyes and I feel exhausted and run down a lot of the time. Life often feels like wading through an endless sea of molasses. For Jack on the other hand, life is one big joy. Every morning at sunrise he wakes up singing his repertoire of film scores and theme tunes. He truly relishes the day ahead at college. Jack is full of life and vitality. He's somebody who relishes the prospect of his routine and also being in the company of his mum and dad who love him dearly.

I'm a bit different. Most mornings I wake up with an intense feeling of dread and an overwhelming fatigue. I dread having to make small-talk at work, of being overloaded with sensory information on the shop floor and most of the time I fantasise about retreating permanently to a remote hilltop monastery in Tibet, shaving my head, throwing on an orange robe and contemplating my breath in solitude for the rest of my days. I hate dealing with the extraneous crap of everyday life and oftentimes I get resentful at having to live in a way that I find unnatural. Such a mode of being is not exactly conducive to good mental health. This unsurprisingly explains why I am on a regular dose of antidepressants and rarely make any friends. Jack makes my parents happy, despite the challenges with which his condition presents them. It was a real battle for them to get him the help he needs but now he has a stable environment, he's no trouble at all. I make my parents worried and miserable. They had very high hopes for me given that I was gifted academically, but I've capitulated in too many instances to negative emotions brought on by a haunting sense of inadequacy, isolation and despair. When Jack and I are together, we're best pals. I don't think there's been a single time we've resented one another's company. Nowadays, we live apart but live fairly close by and see each other once a fortnight. We'll go out together for a bite to eat, a coffee and maybe even a film at the pictures. We don't communicate conventionally through language but we have an unmistakably fraternal bond and what I can only describe as a kind of spiritual connection. Jack smiles at me with his big brown eyes and I smile back with mine. We stick to our usual lunch at the local Portuguese café and both enjoy a cappuccino afterwards. Drinking coffee together makes us feel civilised and, dare I say, normal. We both enjoy being like that from time to time. On the way home, we'll go through the "schoolboy buzzer" routine several times before it's time to say goodbye for another two weeks.

5 – AUTISTIC PEOPLE DON'T LACK EMPATHY

One myth about autistic people that really, really annoys me is that we lack empathy, as though we're all ice-cold psychopaths who go about life with zero concern for the feelings of others. Let me clarify something. This is utterly false. Jack and I may appear distant and withdrawn at times, in a state some less sympathetic psychologists might describe as "morbid self-absorption", but that's not to say that we aren't attuned to the rich emotional worlds of those around us. In spite of our deep preference for personal space and our general aversion to large social gatherings, we are often deeply aware of the suffering in the world, so much so that it can be overwhelming and thus lead to feelings of exhaustion and withdrawal. When I was a child, I remember reacting badly to tragic events appearing before me on the news. Sights of famine in Ethiopia left indelible marks on my mind and were hard to shake off. Upon witnessing such utter misery and despair, I could not understand why those around me weren't reacting hysterically at the sight of skeletal children, too frail to stand or to speak. It affected me on a much more profound level than my peers, I think.

During my childhood, my great-aunt Colleen would often take me to the West End theatre district in London to see a show and it was during these trips that my deep concern for the wellbeing of others and extreme sensitivity to the sights of suffering became apparent to those around me. I remember very fondly taking the Tube from Epping at the end of the Central Line all the way to Tottenham Court Road. At the time, there were several buskers and beggars at the station whom I could barely take my eyes off. I must have been 7 or 8 at the time but I remember the intense feeling of worry I had that the man sitting cross-legged on the floor, wrapped in stained blankets and rattling a paper cup only to be met with the cruel indifference of passers-by, and the feeling that this was deeply wrong and unjust. I fretted that perhaps these poor people, like those in East Africa on the television, might starve to death and that nobody around would so much as bat an eyelid. In my mind, I had to be the one to help these neglected, hunched figures with unkempt beards and gloves full of holes.

For each homeless person we passed, I begged Auntie Colleen for a £2 coin to give to them. Having no conception of money at that tender age, I assumed that this would be enough for them to buy a slap-up meal and a night's stay in a hotel. By about the seventh beggar, my poor old aunt had become somewhat exasperated to say the least, but, even if it was just to placate me, she kept doling out coins which I would then dispense gleefully to those living on the platform. My altruism must have left us penniless by the end of the outing! As I got older, I of course became a little savvier where money's concerned, but that strong feeling of wanting to alleviate the suffering of others has never left me. My daily feeding of local wildlife is testament to this.

Jack's concern for others is similarly strong, especially towards his dear mother. If ever she's upset, he can instantly sense it and he proceeds to stare at her with the most concerned of expressions. If ever she's crying, he whips out a tissue and wipes away her tears. It clearly pains him to see her sad or worried. One incident that we can all recall vividly as a family is one that prompted Jack to express empathy in a way we'd never thought he could. You see, Jack doesn't communicate verbally as we do. He can utter single words and basic phrases, but his ability to construct spontaneous sentences is limited. Maybe the capacity is buried deep in him somewhere and he just hasn't discovered it yet, but who knows? Only he does, I guess. In any case, there was an exception to this that sticks in our minds very vividly for the mere fact it was so unusual of him. It was a Saturday and we'd invited my grandmother around for tea and cake. She'd brought her dog Henry, a lovable but occasionally temperamental Tibetan terrier who had a tendency to snap. Every time he came, we had to make sure to keep him away from our equally if not more temperamental cat Smokey who, like any animal, liked to defend his territory ruthlessly and jealously. On this occasion, we must have been fairly lax and allowed Smokey to creep into the living room in which we were all gathered. Oblivious to our cat's entrance, we suddenly heard a piercing screech and a chorus of growls and hisses. As we turned around, we saw Smokey, an occasionally vicious animal, claws-deep in Henry's neck about to tear the poor dog to shreds. Instinctively, mum jumped in to break up the scrap and in the process got her wrist slashed by our cat's razor-sharp claws. Blood was everywhere and mum was evidently in a state of shock. It had all happened so quickly it was difficult for us all to process. Jack was mortified to see his mother in this condition and, after the bleeding was under control, came up to her and uttered the words: "Are you okay, mum?" Never before had he uttered such a spontaneously constructed sentence. Only the sight of his mother in pain prompted him to go beyond what he is usually comfortable doing. It was a remarkable moment that proved to me that autistic people, even those as disabled as Jack, have a deep reservoir of feeling that occasionally spills out in the most heartfelt of gestures.

cup of tea

6 – AUTISTIC FOOD PREFERENCES

When I was a baby, I was a notoriously fussy eater. My parents would tear their hair out about what it was they were going to feed me. Meal times were exceptionally distressing for all involved. Pureed meals that would easily slip down the hatch of most babies regularly ended up on walls, floors, carpets and people's faces. To get me to eat anything at all proved trickier than convincing an inveterate vegan to eat at a steakhouse. How is it then that I ended up becoming the complete reverse of this in childhood? God only knows.

As I grew out of the baby stage, I became fascinated by the huge variation of cultures and cuisines on earth. One area of the world fascinated me in particular and that was China, a place where they eat practically anything and few foods are taboo. In Guangdong, the region of China from which most of Britain's Chinese population hail, the motto is "Eat anything that moves". I guess it was this philosophy of culinary adventurism that I appropriated from the Cantonese at a very early age.

During our family trips to Chinatown, I would gawk at the often strange and at times slightly terrifying animal carcasses that hung in restaurant windows. Fluorescent orange squid, shiny lacquered ducks and trays of red braised pig entrails heightened my proclivity towards the dark side, that is to say, the stuff to which most Westerners would be naturally averse. My predilection for the bizarre and exotic led me to want to try items of food with which even the bravest of adults might struggle. At age 7, I had tasted stir-fried tripe, smoked duck tongues and pig offal soup.

Living in proximity to London, the place where every ethnic cuisine from every corner of the planet is represented, I was able to satiate my intense desire to eat my way through the vast gamut of world cuisines. Having a mother who shares my passion for food and the literature of Anthony Bourdain enabled me to devour greedily anything I wanted within reason. My mother is adventurous and encouraged me to adopt a similar appreciation of the rich kaleidoscope of human culture. She would take me as a young boy on the Tube to the now derelict ruin which was once the 'Yaohan Plaza', an oriental-style shopping mall in North London, the Japan Centre in Piccadilly and the international food court in Selfridges. My fondest experience was eating my first oyster with her at the seafood bar. It partially grossed me out and partially thrilled me to know that I was eating a live creature. From then on, I've never looked back. It was like an initiation for me into the world of gastronomy. I believe it was these formative experiences that led me to eventually go and live in China for almost two years. Part of my time was spent in the southern province of Fujian, a region of China close to Guangdong with its famous "eat anything that moves" motto. Naturally the opportunities for culinary adventure were abundant there. My first foray into the truly strange and wonderful was in the city of Xiamen (the port city once known as Amoy). It was at an uninviting-looking food stand by the sea that my guide Tam introduced me to sea worms in jelly. Think jellied eels, but with worms. To be honest, it was better than it looked. Even seasoned Chinese gourmets are a little perturbed by this peculiar delicacy I was told, but to me this wasn't so much of a big deal. Tam, my Chinese guide and himself a maniacal foodie, was impressed by my lack of disgust, something he'd expected his Western guest to display. The second speciality I was introduced to by Tam just a few metres from where I'd eaten the worm jelly was a bit more extreme. It was a fertilised chicken egg with a stillborn foetus inside. The egg which was grilled on a filthy little street barbecue by an equally grubby street vendor, was a bloody, feathery little ball that even I struggled with. Still, I showed pluck, if you will excuse the pun, and ate the damn thing in two mouthfuls. It certainly isn't something for the faint-hearted, but I managed it. Never again though.

My point is that Jack and I are at extreme ends of the food spectrum so to speak. Whereas I am open to trying absolutely anything, Jack prefers to stick to an unvarying and limited list of preferences. His favourite is chicken nuggets, a food I am quite frankly disgusted by, and chips. The healthiest part of this meal is a side of baked beans which provide him with some much needed fibre, something in which his diet is worryingly lacking. As he's got older, he's also accepted foods that are similar in shape and overall appearance to his beloved nuggets. These include potato croquettes and fish fingers. He'll also occasionally eat pizza but is quite fussy about the cheese on top. For some strange reason he absolutely adores taramasalata, the strong-tasting pink-coloured fish paste. In fact, my mum and dad had to ration it after it emerged that he was secretly eating it after having had his dinner. At one stage, he'd become quite overweight and we realised the fact that his tub of taramasalata kept going down so rapidly might have had something to do with it! Thankfully he's back to a much healthier weight now due to rationing of the fattening fish paste and the exercise regimen at the college he attends. He even eats a banana and an apple a day which is marvellous. Getting Jack to even taste a vegetable other than a baked bean still proves a tremendous challenge however. I've tried numerous times in vain only to make him gag.

pizza

7 – AN AUTISTIC SENSE OF STYLE

Dressing to impress is a notion to which I have a deep and instinctive aversion. Clothes to me only serve two purposes: to keep you warm and to prevent you from offending the general public. The idea that they can be a way to express one's personality is superficial bordering on nonsensical. They're merely pieces of woven fabric to me. They do nothing to enhance a person's intellect, wisdom or goodness, at least not in my eyes. The fact that "looking good" plays such an important role in our society is something I generally abhor. Wearing a snazzy bow tie does not make one a more learned professor just as having a Jermyn Street suit tailor-made to enhance your figure does not make you savvier at conducting business transactions.

This is why throughout my life I've perhaps rather arrogantly considered myself above having to dress either smartly or in a way that might make me presentable, dare I say, attractive to a member of the opposite sex. Try as I might, I just can't summon the energy to care. In fact I care so little that even at the ripe old age of 29, my dear old nan is still buying me clothes from the local supermarket. Although I am grateful, it's an effort to say thank you given my complete lack of enthusiasm for the way I present myself to others. Sometimes when she buys me clothes, I don't even bother taking off the labels.

One time as a child, I went on a camping holiday to Dorset with my best friend Stuart and his dad. My parents trusted me for the first time in my life to pack my bag. This, unsurprisingly, proved to be a fatal mistake. So blasé was I shoving clothes into my holdall that, instead of packing socks, I mistakenly packed a load of dish cloths. As a matter of necessity, I had to wrap two of these white cloths around my feet in preparation for our 6-mile hiking trip around Corfe Castle. What a wally! Stuart's dad was no doubt bemused but had grown used to my eccentric habits and let me do as I pleased.

Family photos of ours include me in the oddest clothing ensembles. Perhaps the only items of clothing that I liked as a kid were football shirts. In fact, I had quite the collection from practically every city to which my parents had travelled. I would wear a Borussia Dortmund top during trips to the theatre with my old aunt, a Real Madrid shirt to a nice restaurant and a fluorescent green Manchester United jersey to a church service on a Sunday. This multi-coloured array of football shirts was quite often worn together with my favourite pair of comfortable and loose-fitting burgundy jogging bottoms and a pair of leather school shoes. It did not matter to me that others thought I looked ridiculous. In fact, it was my act of rebellion against fashion, both mainstream and alternative.

My brother on the other hand always looks smart and well-groomed. He appreciates nice clothes and always looks tidy and presentable as well as confident in his outward appearance. His wardrobe is full of clothes from Next and he has a penchant for beads and surfer necklaces. Jack's a cool dude, way cooler than me and far more able than I am to pull off sartorial elegance. I guess he takes after my mum and dad who are both naturally good dressers. My whole family in fact has a natural affinity for classic, timeless style. Each time we went on holiday to Italy, mum would take Jack to a Lacoste boutique shop and buy him a new top. His favourite colour is light blue which suits him perfectly.

It's funny because I think if Jack had been born able to lead a conventional life, he would have been a popular extrovert with lots of friends and girlfriends. Even as a very disabled autistic person, he's still in many ways a popular extrovert, expressing himself confidently in his sophisticated sense of dress. His openness and relaxed demeanour also attract others to him whereas I am at the extreme end of introversion. My lack of willingness to retreat outside the realm of imagination and intellect and even dip my toe into the material world tends to be a

shoes

turn-off to most neurotypicals. For all the abundant skill I have with language, I am in many ways a dreadful communicator. It's only as I've matured and in many ways become less self-absorbed that I've realised that being a functional part of human society is reliant on sometimes sacrificing a bit of your authentic self and attempting to please others. Autistic people like me are often fiercely individualistic and sometimes even hostile to any intrusion by outside influences. Although I've remained unencumbered by the pressure to conform socially, I've started to realise that in a cooperative society, presenting oneself to others is important, especially if you wish to receive something in return. Now, that might seem blindingly obvious if you're a neurotypical or even a fellow autistic reader, but to me, it never even entered my mind at any stage until quite recently that perhaps if I were actually to get that job I wanted, I might have to contemplate buying a decent suit that I would be able to wear again to future interviews. If I wanted to make friends or at least establish some sort of connection with others, I might have to wear outfits that the group with which I was keeping company might deem acceptable or at least not consider completely embarrassing.

Even though nan still buys me clothes, they're decent ones that, despite hardly being the crème de la crème of fashion, look half-acceptable for someone of my age. Out of respect for her, I have also, albeit begrudgingly, begun to match my clothes for the first time ever. I'll always remain kind of scruffy, I guess, but as long as Jack's there to give me a piece of fashion advice or two, I'll do my best to heed it.

8 – BULLYING

Confronting our demons is one of the most necessary things we must do as human beings. Hiding away and retreating into a protective bubble is one of the most harmful things we can do to our minds and bodies long-term. As visionary psychoanalyst Carl Jung said "What you resist, persists." Demons that aren't slain lurk in the recesses of your mind and will keep coming back to haunt you. I've realised this late on but I know now that being completely honest about everything is the only way to be for optimum wellbeing.

At school, I suffered a lot of bullying and teasing, from which I had no idea how to defend myself. In fact, I didn't even understand the function of picking on others. Why were these kids in the playground saying nasty things, stealing my backpack and pushing me around? What utility was there in that? This is how my autistic mind works. It's a logic processor that fails to compute rascality. It sees patterns within patterns within yet more patterns. The whole notion of targeting somebody did not fit into any pattern I was able to discern at the time and subsequently caused me much distress.

The bullying really got bad in secondary school when I was about 15 or so. A really nasty kid called Lewis saw me, a chubby, nerdy and potentially vulnerable boy as easy prey. He wound me up by saying "fatty" each time the teacher called my name in the register. I reacted awkwardly and rather embarrassingly in front of the class by saying with characteristic Aspergian earnestness: "Why do you feel the need to keep saying this?" His acolytes, who all grinned inanely at me, would burst out laughing. The whole class, like sheep in a flock, followed suit. I must have sounded stuffy and pompous to them and it was this ability to elicit mindless laughter from the class that I eventually realised was why he did it. He craved attention, because he himself was a wretched, insecure individual. His parents were divorced which clearly troubled him and he was, quite frankly, stupid. I mean really stupid. He was barely able to write a complete sentence without help from the classroom assistant. At the time, I just thought he was evil. I had no appreciation of the fact he was projecting his own inadequacies onto me.

Things got really serious when Lewis burned a big hole in my school blazer with a lit splint during Chemistry class. Our blazers were deadly flammable things and could have easily gone up in flames in a matter of seconds. The Chemistry teacher ignored it and my plea for Lewis to be punished, believing his lie that it was merely an accident. Of course, it wasn't. When I reported the incident to the headmaster, even he did not want to side with me out of a fear of offending the mother of poor, troubled Lewis whom she insisted was an angel. It was during this time that I felt betrayed and unable to trust anyone. This led me to retreat inwards and hide from the outside world. I started flunking exams. During my Physics GCSE, I even ran away and drove my car 100 miles north to Leicester. At university, I hid in my room and subsequently failed my degree. Maybe this wasn't all the fault of the bullying, but I think it played a big part in my gradual breakdown at 21.

Nowadays at 28, I'm learning to do what Carl Jung said was essential for one's psychic health which is to "integrate the shadow". In other words, one has to embrace a part of one's crueler nature in order not to be a pushover. Doing so gives you the strength and the courage to slay demons like bullies and to go confidently into the chaos of existence without resorting to fear and eventual shutdown. Being a bit of a bastard, or at least integrating a bit of your inner bastard into your character is important if you want to defend yourself against those possessed by malice and resentment.

Recently a self-described "intersectional feminist" tried it on with me, claiming that I was bigoted for something that I said on Twitter. She launched into a vicious, ad hominem tirade about me being a "white supremacist" a "misogynist" and other epithets that have no basis in reality. Whereas before I might have cowered away, not being somebody who relishes conflict, this time I was going to nip it in the bud once and for all. I fought back. After a long, mindless scuffle, I blocked and reported the individual. No luck. Determined to slay this demon, I contacted my local constabulary who filed a report for a possible hate crime. My local police station contacted the individual's local police station and they're due to pay her a visit any time soon. I am relishing the shock it is going to give her for what she put me through.

I've since forgiven Lewis for the hell he put me through and I sincerely wish him the best in life. I don't feel resentment towards him. As for the bullying feminist? She deserves exactly what's coming to her and I hope a visit from two coppers will snap her out of her ideological possession. You may be wondering why I haven't mentioned Jack in all this? Well, Jack is too innocent to be bullied. A person would have to have a heart made of stone to ever target him and, if ever they did dare do such a thing, they'd have my wrath and possibly my first fist to incur first.

Jack's a cool dude. I'm a nerdy guy. When mum and dad brought us both a pair of roller blades, it's not hard to guess which one of us was able to skate and which one nearly ended up in the Serpentine lake! This was 15 or so years ago, but I remember the day as though it were yesterday. We'd made a special trip to London's Hyde Park to try out these flashy new inline skates dad had bought us both. Being a nervous and risk-averse child, I was terrified by them. I did the Aspergian thing of catastrophising the event, in this case, envisioning myself losing my balance, falling over and dislocating my elbow. Either that or ending up careening into a group of innocent, unsuspecting Japanese tourists. Jack on the other hand was ready and raring to go. The concept of fear and potential danger is basically alien to him.

After a few minutes walking, we'd found a big wide stretch of tarmac to try out our new skates. By this time, I was nearly in tears. My anxiety was through the roof. To be honest, I was a wimpy kid. Mum once made the error of taking me to a karate class in the hope of toughening me up. Never again. I howled and howled until she could no longer stand the embarrassment of it all.

Once dad had strapped our skates on, we were off. Well,

rOLLy
skeats

Jack was at least. I began with extreme caution, holding on to the adjacent iron railings for dear life. Mum and dad were laughing hysterically while I became increasingly indignant. I must have looked pretty daft whimpering whilst essentially trying to walk on roller blades. By contrast, Jack was having a whale of a time gliding across the park with the confidence of a seasoned professional. As soon as he'd found his rhythm, there was no stopping him. I mean literally, my dad had to run like mad to catch him and physically stop him before he ended up at Marble Arch! Meanwhile, I was still gripping the iron fence.

You can tell just from seeing Jack's friendly and open face that he's never once in his life worried, fretted or panicked. He rarely shows any hints of stress. The reason he was such a natural at rollerblading is that there is no anticipation of potential threats in his mind. Crippling fear is one of the things that holds us all back at some point in our lives. More often than not, the fear is greatly exaggerated in our own minds. In my case, I have long been a persistent worrier and, over time, this has spiralled into anxiety and depression, both of which I wouldn't wish upon my worst enemy. I mean really, they are both truly evil, disgusting illnesses which grow and fester if you don't keep them under control. It's not really surprising that I became ill given that 50% of people with

Asperger's suffer from depressive disorders of some sort. We can blame society for not making the correct accommodations for us, but I tend to believe that this is an inherent and inescapable part of our condition. Neuroscientists point to the fact this may be because individuals with Asperger's Syndrome tend to have larger amygdalae, the part of the brain that processes emotions like fear, than the neurotypical population.

The only time I ever see Jack in a state one might describe as anxious is when his sacred routine is interrupted in some way. If ever there's a Bank Holiday and his college is shut for the day, my parents at home have a hard time trying to explain to him why this is the case. He thrives on regularity, consistency and routine and, whenever this pattern is disturbed, he displays flashes of agitation which he expresses through "stimming" behaviours such as hand-flapping or rocking back and forth on his bed. When he's anxious about his routine being out-of-sync, these behaviours become more vigorous. If ever we're sitting in the lounge, we hear Jack's bed and the floorboards above us creaking as he rocks back and forth, sometimes for hours. This is very normal to us but I can understand why to outsiders, without any experience of autistic behaviour, this might seem strange and even a little disturbing. We know however that this is just Jack's thing. It's his way of regulating his emotional wellbeing and his nervous system.

Before autism was even recognised, the physical quirks of people like Jack would have been viewed as pathological and stimming would have no doubt been discouraged, even 'treated'. Once upon a time, we as a family were painfully self-conscious about his behaviour while out in public and we lived in constant fear of him being stared at, mocked or derided. It wasn't nice. Fortunately, attitudes towards autistic individuals have become more accepting since the time Jack was a child and his stimming behaviours were much more "severe". One thing I suppose Jack has made us realise as a family is not to pay any attention to what others think. It's simply not worth the aggravation. We've appropriated a bit of Jack's fearlessness in that respect. Indeed, if only we could all be as fearless as he is, the world would be a much happier, less divided place. People might have greater courage and would do the things they'd been meaning to but had long put off out of a fear of what others thought or the potential risk it might involve. The world could learn a lot from my brother which is why I'm writing about him now. He can't communicate as we do but I know he'd appreciate me sharing his way of being with you all.

Our family's Catholic for the most part. We're not exactly churchgoing types, but culturally we're still very Catholic. My mum has a strong conscience and an abiding sense of duty towards family which are both fundamentally Catholic values. Like me, she's a sceptic about dogma and theology, but in terms of acting out a Christian metaphysic, she's unmistakably Christ-like and I mean that from the bottom of my heart. What my mum has had to put up with, what with raising one very disabled son was not easy and required a lot of love and courage to survive. Facing a cold and indifferent system that did not exactly provide adequate care and support for Jack only added to my mum's struggle. Through sheer stoicism and a faith that goodness would eventually prevail, we've all come out the other end as a strong, united family bound by compassion and a sense of looking after one another which sustains us through the challenges with which life presents us daily.

In terms of our beloved Catholic saints, both mum and I are very close to St. Francis of Assisi, patron saint of animals. I'm a great admirer of the Buddha who shares a lot of parallels with Catholicism's great mystics like St. Francis. In fact, it is possible St. Francis came into contact with Eastern ideas brought by travelling Buddhist monks,

Hindu sages and Sufi mystics during his time in Alexandria. It was on encountering these ideas that he felt inspired to seek a more inward-looking spiritual style that relied less on dogma and more on direct experience. This led him into seclusion, away from the trappings of man-made artifice and into nature where, for extended periods he communed with wildlife, especially the birds. My mum is just like him. She's perhaps less friendly with the birds, but in our house not a day goes by without them being fed. Filling up the seed trays and peanut boxes is a daily ritual at home and one that has an unmistakably Franciscan flavour about it. In addition, we also feed a family of foxes in the evening who arrive more or less at the same time to feast on a three-course meal of dog food, eggs and sometimes even chicken legs. We spoil them because we love animals as fellow sentient beings. How anyone could be cruel to such splendid creatures, is beyond our comprehension.

I take after mum in many respects. It's therefore unsurprising that I've carried on this quasi-religious animal-feeding ritual in my own home and that, like my mum, I eventually went on to become a vegetarian (albeit one who slips from time to time). The thought of animals in distress causes me a lot of pain, so much so that I even tried out veganism for a period. As noble endeavour as it seemed, the lure of stinky gruyere and runny, oozy camembert was just too much.

Jack by contrast is far less fussed about animals. It's perhaps not so much that he dislikes them but that in his relentlessly structured autistic worldview, animals don't serve any rational purpose. They don't fit neatly and succinctly into a conceptual box like, say, a chair does. Their behaviour to his mind is strange, chaotic, feckless and hard to fathom. Barney, our miniature Schnauzer who frequently tries to initiate play with Jack, is rebuffed or, more often than not, simply ignored. The dog is as bemused by his behaviour as I think many humans are. Jack's aversion to animals might also be a result of our previous cat, Smokey, who was an especially aggressive little thing even at the best of times. He'd been given to us, funnily enough by Jack's former ABA therapist whose younger siblings threw stones at poor Smokey as a kitten. Due to these traumatic early beginnings, he'd developed a kind of persecution complex and was prone to swipe viciously at you if you approached him at an angle he didn't like or you attempted to rub his belly. The funny thing is he could also be sweet and affectionate, but to Jack, a boy of strict order and continuity, Smokey and his fiery temper were not exactly ideal. When Jack would arrive home from school, he'd throw his coat over him and sprint up the stairs to avoid having his socks slashed by his sharp claws. Jack kept his door closed at all times so as to avoid him intruding on his personal space.

By contrast, Smokey and I got on well and made good friends, even if he did lash out at me a few times. I guess we're both a bit screwed up and, as they say, all cats have Asperger's Syndrome so I guess we're alike in many respects. He sensed we were alike and took an instant shine to me, sitting on my lap every day for an hour while I did my homework. He'd also sleep under the duvet next to me. I dearly loved that cat and haven't quite got over him passing away. To Jack, I'm guessing it made little difference not having him in the house. But who knows for sure?

All I really know is that he most certainly isn't animal-mad like me and mum. At college he does enjoy horse-riding and one time in the Bahamas, he even swam with dolphins. This was when swimming with dolphins was hyped up as the next trendy autism "therapy" based on a few dubious anecdotes about kids whose lives were transformed by the mystical powers of these friendly fish. What a load of old nonsense that proved to be, at least in Jack's case! In reality, the poor dolphins had been snatched from their home in the Atlantic and were being exploited for the amusement of gullible people, mainly

smokey

rich Americans. While in the pool, Jack was quite insistent he did not want to engage with the big, rubbery grey fish flapping around in front of him. I couldn't blame him to be honest. The weird, unearthly clicking sounds the dolphins make were bad enough. The whole event was a farce. In fact, the company that ran the dolphin tours was shut down after complaints of cruelty.

Given Jack's experiences with both an aggressive cat and a giant fish, it's no wonder he opts for an animal-free existence. The thoroughly irritating New-Age idea of animals being able to unlock the spiritual potential of autistic people is just bunk. What an absolute myth! Perhaps some autistic people's lives, especially those that respond well to animals, have been improved substantially just by having a furry companion around, but to suggest that these animals have some sort of healing power or an innate ability to bring autistic people out of their shell is utter claptrap. Like so many other myths that have been spun by the gutter-press, this one is among the most persistent and indeed irritating. Another is the myth that all autistic people have a superpower, for which we all have Dustin Hoffman's 'Rain Man' to thank.

Autism is a very misunderstood condition. The 1988 Oscar-winning film Rain Man features an autistic man played by Dustin Hoffman who, though lacking in basic social skills, is blessed with extraordinary savant abilities in card-counting and complex mental calculation. Unfortunately the film is the sole basis for an alarming number of public perceptions of a condition that can be both challenging and heartbreaking for the parents and relatives of those affected. The reality of autism for the vast majority of people is far more prosaic than Hollywood portrays. In fact, fewer than 8% of those who have this complex life-long neurodevelopmental disorder actually possess savant-like mathematical talents.

My 26-year-old sibling Jack, an angel though he is, will never be able to live the life of an ordinary adult. He will require full-time care for the rest of his life which will necessitate someone keeping his bottom clean. We all love him dearly, but at the same time we are forced to swallow the bitter pill that he will never have a career, a house, a car or a family like the rest of us. This is a tough thing to come to terms with. Sometimes it can be soul-destroying for my parents who never see their son progressing towards a goal. He grows older physically but mentally remains a perpetual infant. This is not an easy thing with rain man

which to come to terms.

St. Elizabeth's, a local college he attends which specialises in the care and education of people with complex learning needs, has provided a lifeline for my parents. It's there that Jack can thrive as a human being in a caring, nurturing environment with staff who are loving, kind and dedicated to helping him and other people like him take part in activities and practical work that give him a sense of purpose and meaning. A lot of the activities they do, such as horse riding, gardening and outdoor pursuits, are run as 'social enterprises'. Jack also spends one day a week working at a local shop which raises funds for the college by selling handmade items of jewellery to the public. For this, he receives a pay packet each week.

His college is an abundantly positive place which gives people like Jack with often very severe types of disability, a place in the world. Moreover, the college treats Jack with the respect and dignity that he deserves by recognising him, not just as a disabled person, but as a valuable member of society who has a lot to contribute. It's astonishing how they've transformed his life and those of his parents for the better through positive engagement. The staff there live and breathe compassion, an ethos that has even rubbed off on Jack who, despite his naïve egocentrism, shows a softer, more caring side to his nature at the college by helping the more disabled pupils to tie their shoelaces. It's a heartening thing for parents and me to hear. Jack has also never been happier or more prosperous and relishes the prospect of getting up, drinking his coffee and hopping into his taxi to go there each morning. Keeping him constantly occupied both physically and mentally is key to managing his condition, and without the stellar work St. Elizabeth's does for him to achieve this, I can't imagine what an uphill struggle life might have been for our family. For one thing, it provides much-needed respite for my embattled parents who, in addition to having a disabled son in Jack, also have a moody and temperamental son in me.

Another myth is that all autistic people are scrupulously honest to the point of rudeness. There is some truth in that, but it would be dishonest of me to say it was the whole truth! It was observed by child developmental psychologist Jean Piaget that clever kids learn to tell lies at a young age, usually to get what they want or to avoid getting into trouble. I was one of those kids. I didn't tell lies in a malicious way, but I'd frequently pretend I'd done my homework when in fact I had been indulging my passion for computer games. I was also a chubby kid who loved eating. The foods I loved were rationed by my parents and rightly so. On my way back from school, I'd buy two chocolate bars and hide behind the bins at Tesco so that I wouldn't be seen by my parents if they happened to have been passing. As I got older, I started to lie about my school grades which were mediocre at best, especially in the subjects I didn't care about like Physics and Chemistry. I even lied about having a girlfriend at one point after I overheard my parents speculating one time whether or not I might be gay. My lying had become a way of maintaining a semblance of normality in a difficult and abnormal situation with Jack. I had to at least appear to be the "normal" one. I started lying to protect myself, but I lied more and more to protect my parents from further hurt caused ironically by the lies I told before. It became a nasty and vicious cycle. I would have loved to have been a nice, well-adjusted young man in whom my parents could have taken pride, but instead my teens were problem-ridden and exacerbated by my dishonesty. I carried on this façade of normality, what Asperger's expert Tony Attwood describes as the "Aspergian mask", for years until it had become pathological in nature. It all came to a head when my parents experienced the horror of finding out that I'd spent my entire final year at university in my room, gorging on fast-food, not turning up to lectures and watching videos on the internet.

I'd become nihilistic, depressed and exhausted as a result

of choosing to retreat into a personal hell of my own making and having to admit all this to my parents was even more hellish. They were too shocked, perhaps even too dismayed, to be angry. It sent my mum into a depression. She felt as though she couldn't get out of bed for a few weeks after. Looking back, I'd become a wicked, self-destructive monster and I'm not proud of it one bit. It's only been in the last year that I've decided to get my life back on track for the sake of my family's whole wellbeing. It has necessitated rewiring my brain in a sense from years of dishonesty and cowardice. Telling the truth at all times is top of my agenda. It's partly why I am writing this now and it's not easy when you've relied on lies to cover up for your own inadequacy for years on end.

But I had to start somewhere if I was to live a healthy and meaningful life. For me, it began with small, incremental changes. I composed a list of everything that I'd kept a secret and needed to get out. I admitted everything about my secret eating to my parents and vowed to stop. I stopped telling my parents I'd gone to work when I hadn't. I admitted that I'd been thoroughly selfish throughout my life and needed for once in my life to cultivate a real sense of responsibility and self-respect in preparation for my parents getting older. I'm still figuring out how to make mum and dad proud, but I'll start by laying the groundwork first. On Monday, I start my new job at Poundland. It's not much, but it's a start.

Most young kids are not preoccupied with order. They are usually quite content to throw their toys around, to leave a huge mess in the kitchen after a cupcake making session or to come home from a football match caked in mud. Autistic kids are different. They don't tend to exhibit the same carefree behaviour as neurotypical kids. When in the playground, the latter will typically form groups, play with one another and cooperate in tasks like building things out of Duplo.

Autistic kids will often cut lonely figures in a playground, appearing aloof and uninterested in who is around them, preferring instead to remain in a secluded corner, stimming or maybe talking to themselves. Playing games with kids requires a lot of abstract thinking and social imagination. Cowboys and Indians would be of little interest to most autistic kids for this reason. They'd more likely enjoy a task that involves both being solitary and arranging objects into some kind of order or pattern. Stacking cans in the kitchen, straightening objects on the dining room table or arranging crayons into separate colours is more 'our thing'. Jack was an archetypal example of the high systemiser.

When my grandmother and Jack were out walking in our

local woodlands, they stopped close to a detached house by the roadside. Nan's dog, Ollie, stopped to relieve himself by a lamppost. Meanwhile, Jack had wandered off without her knowing into the house's front garden which was cluttered with an eclectic assortment of gnomes and ornaments. It must have seemed like absolute anarchy in Jack's mind. So, in a typically autistic fashion, he took it upon himself to start rearranging these objects into some semblance of order, first by setting them in rows along the garden wall. As soon as Ollie was done, Nan turned around and was stunned to see what Jack had done. He'd created what appeared to be a work of art of geometric beauty and precision. At the time, Jack had yet to be diagnosed as autistic although the idea had been put out there by one of the GPs we'd been in contact with. This particular event was one of the catalysts for him receiving the full ASD assessment, so typical was it of autistic behaviour.

What I've noticed about Jack is that everything around him has to be put in its conceptual box so to speak. Everything must be where it should be and any change in that order is met with resistance. If something is taken away, like our cat Smokey, whom he'd got used to as part of the fabric of the household, he gets upset and starts repeating "Where's Smokey? Where's Smokey? Where's

Smokey?" He mitigates the chaos with hand-flapping and rocking. He's also the same when something additional is added, especially when it interrupts his routine or if something comes into the house that shouldn't be there. One of his pet dislikes and something he feels he must correct is an object which might be hanging off the edge of a table. In Jack's mind, this just won't do and must be corrected without a moment's hesitation. Permanently his mind is trying to create order out of chaos which explains why he typically prefers his own company to that of others and sticks to an unvarying diet of college, dinner and videos. The world of human relationships, interpersonal communication and socialising is far too abstract, chaotic and even nightmarish for the relentlessly logical autistic brain to figure out. This is where Jack and I are indeed similar, although our experiences at opposite ends of the autism spectrum have in many ways been radically different.

Like Jack, I prefer to avoid contact with people outside of my own immediate family for the most part, preferring instead to live inside my own head in which I create rich inner-worlds of my own imagination. I would describe myself, not so much as anti-social but as semi-social. Two famous probable Aspergians were the empirical philosophers Immanuel Kant, who would take an afternoon stroll at exactly the same time every day for his whole life, and Jeremy Bentham, who preferred isolation but would occasionally enjoy socialising with others for the health benefits. Both of their lives had, what may seem to neurotypicals to be a cold, calculated feel to them.

I hold my individuality to be sacred and, as much as I hate my ideas becoming too derivative and influenced by others, I do occasionally feel an intense need to bounce my ruminations, meditations and formulations off others in order to get some much-needed perspective on things. Otherwise, I would risk going mad. The result of my interactions with others is often a one-sided monologue which is probably the reason why I've struggled to make friends in the past! A chat with me is usually dominated by exactly what it is I wish to talk about and, if it deviates from my specific area of interest, I have an uncanny ability to steer it back into exactly the direction I want it to go. It's perhaps this lack of appreciation of the listener's own feelings that makes us "Aspies" unpopular in the realm of informal, polite society. Added to that, I am practically blind to facial expressions. I cannot read boredom in a person's face, nor anger nor embarrassment. The concept of body language is one that I also can't easily grasp. Although I have made a concerted effort to improve my social skills, I doubt that I'll ever be at the level of being able to go to a loud, boisterous group event like, say, a stag do. Being in a noisy group environment filled with small-talk leads me to drown in a sea of information. This is when psychosomatic feelings of anxiety come on and my mind goes into full shutdown. It's an unnerving and sometimes quite horrifying experience. This I would say is the most disabling aspect of my Asperger's, but I don't know whether, given the chance, I would change it. It's hard to say because it's a part of me and who I am.

The truth is, I appreciate the fewer but in my mind much more profound one-to-one interactions I have with, say, George, the elderly Sri Lankan man I talk to in the local coffee shop. We both have a shared interest in politics and religion. There's also Dawa, the local postman from Tibet who I chat with for hours about our shared passion for Buddhism. Being autistic requires me to demand a lot of personal space in which I can be my authentic self without the intrusion of the outside world and the exigencies of material existence. That's not to say either Jack or I are hermits, because we're not. We value the company of others; we just don't require it with the same degree of frequency as a neurotypical person does.

My advice to anyone who knows somebody on the spectrum is to allow them to have a decent amount of personal space but not to let them stay there for too long.

Bring them out of their shell from time to time, but don't overwhelm them. Find somewhere roughly in the middle between autistic order and neurotypical chaos in order that they can both be true to themselves and also be relatively functional in society.

13 – AUTISTIC SENSORY CHAOS

It is said that autistic people experience external reality in higher definition than most. A strong sensitivity to touch, bright light and loud noises is a typical trait of autistics across the spectrum. Jack and I are no different in that respect. We both reluctantly shake hands with others and even then we might seek a hand wipe after having done so. We're not big on displays of physical affection either so there's no point in gesturing to hug us because we'll ignore you. Somebody once described hugging me as akin to grabbing onto a piece of wood. I guess it really isn't my thing and Jack is the same. It's not part of our mode of being or of expressing how we feel authentically inside. Speaking for myself, a hug or a hen peck is a superficial and meaningless gesture. It feels more like affectation than genuine affection to me. I don't begrudge others doing it, but it's not for me. More than my sensitivity to touch is my sensitivity to sound which at times is just unbearable and I do mean unbearable. The most dreaded scenario I could imagine is one that involves sudden loud bangs. My nervous system as a whole does not respond well to them.

Fireworks displays as a child were the most terrifying events imaginable to my sensitive system. Before a display, I would grab my father's hand and spend the fireworkes

entire time fretting and praying to God that it would all be over soon. Other kids my age were enjoying themselves meanwhile. Each bang sent a reverberation through me that caused me to experience what I can only describe as pain. My grandmother was the only one who sympathised with me, offering me swigs of whisky from her hip flask as the explosions went on around us. Jack on the other hand loves fireworks. He relishes the loud bangs, the bright electric colours and the atmosphere of the whole spectacle. While he attends a local display with my dad, I'll cower under my bedclothes with ear plugs pressed firmly into my lobes. It's said that all cats have Asperger's Syndrome, or at least according to a book of a similar title. One of the traits we Aspies share with our beloved feline companions is our increased perceptual awareness of sound. On 5th November, my old cat Smokey and I would hide under the duvet next to one another until the cacophony outside was over. Smokey gravitated to me in times of threat or potential danger I think because we shared similarly nervous dispositions. We also dearly loved one another and the day he died I felt very distraught, as though I'd lost a soul mate.

I'm probably at my happiest and most relaxed when I'm stroking a cat. I adore the sensation on my hands of soft, smooth fur and the gentle vibrations that echo through my hands as a cat expresses its appreciation by purring. I find them to be profoundly anxiety reducing creatures on both an emotional and a sensory level which is why I think many Aspies feel a strong connection to them. As far as touching human beings though, it doesn't come quite as naturally to me and nor is it something I'm inclined to do. Recently I received acupuncture which also includes a vigorous back massage to help stimulate blood flow. The sensation of too much touch can be quite overwhelming to my system, much like noise is. As the Chinese doctor put his hands on me and began digging gently into my muscles, I flinched. It was an instinctive reflex and it kept happening. For this reason, he could not carry on with the massage and the 1-hour session had to be ended prematurely. Jack's pretty much the same. He goes out of his way to avoid even the closest relatives touching him. When my grandmother insists she gives him a kiss, instead of offering her his cheek, Jack bows down and gives her a full head of hair for her to peck. I guess it's less sensitive than flesh. We're a peculiar pair. Whenever somebody is too close to our faces when talking, we'll move away from them quite unapologetically. In Jack's case, he's able to get away with it more easily due to him being more obviously disabled than I am. I have to be careful or risk alienating people around me.

One thing Jack does do that has a habit of putting those he comes into contact with on edge is his insistence on tapping a person who may have accidentally bumped into him. I know, it's strange and none of us understands why he does it. It's just one of his many autistic quirks. It may not make any rational sense but then again, neither do many of the rituals involved in conventional organised religion. Tapping someone is as important to him as saying prayers to a man in the sky is to a believer. In any case, it goes to show that human beings, whether autistic or neurotypical, do bizarre things to make order out of chaos and to attempt to put up a perceptual frame in front of the unknown.

Jack's most prized possession, in addition to his laptop on which he watches all his favourite films, is his pair of flashy headphones. It is with the aid of these miraculous things that he is able to tune out of the exterior world or arbitrary noise and into one in which he knows exactly what's coming next. Every time one of us sticks our head around his bedroom door to check up on him, he's got them on and appears immersed in his own private realm of comforting familiarity. I wear a much less flashy pair to tune out the clanking and whirring of the washing machine downstairs. If I'm working or trying to concentrate on reading a good book, even the sound of my

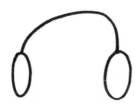

head pohes

neighbour opening and closing her wheelie bin in the evening can be disturbing. On a Friday evening when my other neighbour will often decide to host a party, headphones become a necessity for the entire evening or else be tormented by the horror of incessant chatter, clinking beer bottles, thumping bass, blaring synthesisers and slamming doors. I would definitely not cope well without them.

Sensory issues are no trivial thing for autistic folk. Although treatments are frowned upon by some members of our community, especially those who pride themselves on their autistic identity, I would welcome the chance to reset my sensory receivers to a more muted tone. As I get older, my sensitivity to being in loud venues seems to be getting a lot worse, too. This is no good for somebody like me who is frequently told needs to try to "get out more".

The ability to focus on one thing and one thing only for extended periods of time is a particular strength of the autistic mind. Whereas the neurotypical mind is easily distracted by external stimuli and the insatiable urge to be social, those on the spectrum can spend long durations in complete isolation oblivious to anything else and entirely focussed on a single object of meditation. It's an extraordinary ability to have especially when coupled with a keen intellect, even if it is often to the detriment of a conventional lifestyle in which one takes the time to enjoy the company of others, the simple pleasures of preparing a meal or taking one's children to the park.

To an obsessively driven autistic mind, the intense, even maniacal levels of attention paid to a special interest far supersedes the need to partake of the "real world" which can often seem like a persistent irritant that gets in the way. When autistic people are fully engaged, they feel completely immersed in a world that makes complete sense to them, where the distinction between object and subject of the meditation dissolves temporarily. It's a remarkable transformation that occurs when autistic people who are highly focussed are allowed to express their true selves. I guess the neurotypical mind will always consider such behaviour strange and alien but it's okay, because the daily need for inane, superficial chatter is equally puzzling to our minds. Perhaps we'll never truly be able to understand our respective ways of being, but that's fine. All we ask is that we are allowed the space every now and then to lose ourselves in a spiritual, trance-like state where time and space drift away into vague abstractions and we become momentarily fused with our divine nature.

These spiritual states aren't always easy to reach, but every autistic person I've spoken to can identify in some way with a time they've felt so engaged in something that they consider to be meaningful that they experience a kind of dopaminergic rush akin to ecstasy. The way in which autistic people describe these inner-states of bliss and tranquility can sound maddeningly vague to others, especially to those who prefer to attend to the practical concerns of the everyday. I get that. Anyway, autistic people should never aspire to remain in such states of inner-bliss and ought always to be encouraged first to do what is necessary in the practical realm before ascending into higher-consciousness.

For me, I remember reaching such a state in my room when I began the serious business of learning a language from scratch. For the best part of a week, I did almost nothing other than internalising the patterns of German grammar, harmonising them in my mind until they became a part of me and then enriching these structures with pages and pages of vocabulary which I was able to soak up like a sponge. Carl Jung describes the phenomenon of synchronicity when all previously disparate elements merge into a seamless, multi-layered composition that then fills you with a kind of religious awe. In that week, I defied conventional logic and reason by teaching myself to speak a language fluently and with a degree of proficiency comparable to that of a native speaker. My method was highly intuitive, unconventional and relied on my uncanny talent for filtering only the necessary information required to begin a cumulative process of mental construction. Our German teacher at the time was stunned by my rapid progress. This progress ensured that I was picked along with a few other high-achieving German students to take part in an 8-week exchange with a prestigious school in Frankfurt. There I was able to blend in with German life as though I had been born into a German family. It was almost eerie for others to behold. There was simply no trace of my English background in my German-speaking voice. When I returned to England, one teacher evidently felt threatened by this and began accusing me of cockiness when I started to correct his errors. At the time, I assumed I was helping him and the thought that I was undermining his authority never occurred to me, not being one predisposed to such a desire for hierarchy and dominance myself.

My brother Jack shares similar traits though our abilities are indeed very different. He's a bit more like a recording device which, unlike my ability with German, isn't of any great use to society. It's charming and funny, but that's not to say it's savant-like. Autism can in some cases confer great benefits and distinctive strengths, but that is not to say people like Jack are endowed with these special and unusual talents. As I am writing this, I am acutely aware that claiming Jack possesses some kind of autistic superpower would be a lie and quite a dangerous one at that. Many in the advocacy communities and networks are keen to highlight the distinctive talents of autistic people which I do think is admirable and well-intentioned, at least for the most part. That's not to say however that it's realistic. Some autistic people certainly are talented. Take Stephen Wiltshire, the "human camera" who draws entire cityscapes in minute detail from memory, or the Maths genius Daniel Tammet. These are rare examples of course, but the idea that autism is a strength neglects the reality that a large number are so disabled both physically and mentally as to be actually quite tragic.

Fortunately, though Jack is severely autistic, he has a truly exceptional personality which brings joy to us all. I believe his lovable nature is independent of his disability. I've met some autistic people who are quite aggressive, sometimes violent, self-injurious and completely unable to relate in any way to others. Those trying to see autism entirely through rose-tinted specs tend to ignore the uncomfortable truth that those who are severely affected possess few attributes we can call positive. Of course, they are loved by their families. That is beyond question, but to accuse the parents of such children who advocate for a cure of being inhumane is dishonest and morally reprehensible in my view. As a mildly autistic man with a very disabled brother, I simply can't ignore this big elephant in the room. Autism may be an identity-label to some, especially those who are like me and have huge potential that isn't realised partly due to stigma, but to many it is a crippling disorder which causes great suffering to those affected.

I really, really wish I could say Jack has some sort of superpower, but alas, he hasn't and for that I am actually quite grateful. I wouldn't want him to become a kind of circus freak for the media to gawk over and profit from. I love him how he is and despite the challenges we all face as a family because of his disability. Journalists may want to write about Jack's ability to memorise entire film scripts, but I doubt it will be of much interest to serious people.

It may provide a minute's entertainment to a casual internet reader, but that's about it. My brother's autism is certainly not a source of amusement to my parents who have to hear Terry Thomas hundreds of times over every day or to my father who has to keep his bottom clean as a result of his incontinence.

When I see a lot of the left-wing posturing online about autism being an identity as opposed to a disability, I grind my teeth a little and seethe with righteous indignation. The radical activists rarely know what autism is like for the parents of profoundly disabled kids.

eLPhenPNt inthe rom

15 – AUTISTIC SINGLE-MINDEDNESS

I don't like being bitter, but sometimes I can't help it. When you've lived on the fringes of society feeling as though you don't really belong, it's easy to become a tad resentful at times. I could have easily become part of the victimhood mob that classifies autistic people as an oppressed group in society and rant incessantly about rights and privileges. But I don't believe we're oppressed. I just think people don't understand us. This is why I write because I believe that it is through the medium of storytelling that human beings learn best. We're not naturally logic processors who learn by facts and reason alone. Stories feed our imagination and empathy, the parts of our brain that help us conceptualise the world better than any science. But for these stories to have a genuine meaning at all, I have to be totally honest and transparent about every detail. I don't have an agenda to espouse other than to give you a window into my way of seeing things, both about myself and my brother. This takes a surprising amount of courage because expressing inconvenient truths about autism to those who want to believe it is merely a benign difference rather than a disability in all those who have the condition, inevitably leads to me being shunned by those who may have shown support in the past. Luckily, I'm immune to the groupthink and herd mentality of many autism groups and I attribute this ironically to my being autistic and having a relentlessly individual nature. People call me arrogant which may to some extent be true, but I always maintain the possibility I may be wrong in some of the things I say and am never averse to changing my mind provided my reason and my conscience agree. For some, maintaining distance from teams and groups and being an individual is an uncomfortable mind-set within which to live, but I would rather sacrifice the security the group offers for the sake of what I believe to be true.

I suspect many whistle-blowers in history were autistic or at least had autistic traits. Truth is held up as an almost sacred value in the minds of many autistic people I have met and the inherent insistence on being honest often ends up being to the detriment of social relationships which rely on group fantasies and the omission of important but inconvenient facts in order to sustain themselves. The singlemindedness and relentless independence of Aspergians is something from which I think society as a whole may benefit.

There is something so pure about Jack you can almost feel a bit of the divine in him. His ability to diffuse tense situations by saying essentially what's on all our minds often removes the burdens of all the petty fears and apprehensions that divide us. If Jack doesn't want to do something, he'll say so unflinchingly, unencumbered by the worry of what others may think of him. Notions of flattery and sycophancy are alien to his autistic mind.

It would free us of all the neuroses floating around our subconscious minds. That said, it would also alienate us from the groups we rely on for support, companionship and comfort. I guess that we autistics have a higher capacity for being self-sufficient, not being ones to crave collective security as much as neurotypical people, who tend to be more preoccupied with seeking status and validation from those around them.

I guess I'm not at the extreme end of being an isolated individual like some autistic people I know or have heard about who have no contact with others and prefer to remain that way. My companions are not always objects and special interests. I'm a semi-social creature who likes interaction infrequently, perhaps once a week, and even then it has a stilted and formal quality to it. My verbal ability enables me to give off the appearance of being quite mainstream, though this is often at odds with my true nature. I don't like the pretence of social interaction generally and, not having that vital interlocutor between brain and mouth like a lot of people, I am liable to say things that offend. This meant having few close friends as a child and a string of angry ex-friends in adulthood. I regularly upset people with my at times direct style of communication and by obeying truth over people's feelings. This is often construed as a lack of empathy on my part, which as I explained earlier, is a simplistic view which neglects my deep compassion for those in need.

In the past, I've been referred to as a hermit owing to my singular and reclusive lifestyle which often puts me at odds with those around me. I compare myself favourably to the American transcendentalist philosopher Thoreau who renounced community for a secluded and ascetic lifestyle in the woods. It's not to say I don't often think about living at least some semblance of a conventional lifestyle, but somehow I don't feel marrying or having kids would come naturally to someone of my temperament. Jack and I can both be stubborn and difficult so-and-sos at times. I can understand the exasperation of others when either of us is in a particularly petulant and pigheaded mood. When Jack is sitting in the car, he does his usual thing of muttering bits of film script to himself. When he continues to repeat the same thing over and over, it really does start to grate on all of us. He picks up on this frustration in all of us and begins to do it more and more, particularly when we're in the car and stuck in traffic. Usually one of us snaps by uttering a loud "shoosh!"

Jack, despite being far more disabled, is in many ways far less of a problem than me when it comes to temperament. Being highly anxious and not emotionally stable, I have a tendency towards "meltdowns", to which autistic people are often prone. This is where one negative emotion catalyses a whole host of other negative emotions and eventually spirals into an outburst of anger followed by depression and usually streams of tears. It's not pretty or dignified and it can leave me feeling highly embarrassed and ashamed afterwards. In Asperger's, the emotional switch is turned up perpetually to full volume which probably accounts for such events which are, unfortunately in my case, once-weekly occurrences. Just today, despite waking up in a surprisingly good mood, which is rare for me, I received an email from my publisher saying that he was still in the process of editing my first book and that he wasn't sure when it would be published. I was quite narked by the uncertainty of his words and could not stop obsessing over them. The fact that there was no clear deadline put me on edge and pushed me eventually back into an all-too familiar vortex of anger and despair. During a trip out, I vented these feelings in front of my parents in a disgraceful manner. As the anxiety began to wreak havoc on my nervous system,

I spoke recklessly of ditching the whole book-writing endeavour, of giving up on everything and began ranting childishly about my life being over and there being no reason to have any hope for the future. I looked a complete fool.

It was only a few hours after the anxiety and rage had subsided that I began to reassess the situation with a cool and rational head. I was able to see things from my publisher's perspective and was then able to appreciate all the hard work involved on his part. The grip on my own set of narrow self-interests loosened and I started to worry less about the situation. The transformation from impetuous, angst-ridden kid to responsible, mature and level-headed adult was rapid indeed.

happy sad

Jack was always intensely curious as a boy about my facial hair growth as I hit puberty. When I started shaving at 15, he'd stand outside and stare with an intense expression at me as I performed the manly ritual of first rinsing the face with warm water, rubbing foam onto my face and gently gliding a razor across my skin, making sure not to miss any spots under my nose and chin. If ever I forgot to shave, he'd stroke my face and feel the prickly stubble. It fascinated him. I guess he wondered why he himself hadn't grown any yet. That all changed a couple of years later when, after a spurt of hair growth in Jack's moustache area appeared we decided it was time for him to shave.

We eased him in gently by buying an electric razor which he was able to use safely. However, what he wanted more than anything was to experience the full wet shave just as he'd watched me do countless times before. The thought of Jack using a sharp object on himself frightened us a little bit, so I decided one day to shave him myself. He could not have been more appreciative. He stood still and behaved impeccably as I rinsed his face, applied some foam and softly slid the razor under his nose. This was his initiation ceremony into manhood and it was a moment my mum watched from outside with tears streaming down her face. I guess she was feeling mixed emotions. There was a feeling of deep affection and joy at seeing her two sons bonding in such a poignant way, but I imagine this was shot through with an abiding sense of sadness about Jack's uncertain future. Despite the shaving ceremony, my mum was of course painfully aware Jack would not go on to do the other things that make men men. She was reminded in that single instant that he would never have a job, get married or have kids. She was reminded he'd perpetually remain an infant. This feeling haunts us and leads to feelings of depression and disillusionment in each of us from time to time. Even so, we don't allow this to rob us of moments of joy and happiness. Mum always stresses to me the importance of grabbing on to both when they occur as a way of alleviating suffering caused by circumstances outside our control. When we're sitting together as a family in front of the television and Jack says something funny from one of his videos, we make the most of the moment and howl. Having a sense of humour sustains us. It is the mechanism we use to soften the burdens of life.

Sometimes humour among ourselves can be a little dark. For example, the other day Jack had a birthday party at home which we all enjoyed. We had a birthday cake, candles, balloons and colourful bunting adorning the front of the house. It was delightful in its innocence and we all had a wonderful time indulging in finger food and silly party games that evoked a lot of laughter. A few days later we went to visit our old aunt who now lives permanently in a care home. She's profoundly deaf and to make matters worse, she doesn't wear her hearing aids! Having a conversation with her can be an exasperating and at times entirely futile endeavour as she misapprehends nearly every other word you say to her. Naturally, being Jack's great aunt, she wanted to know about his birthday celebrations and what presents he received. Mum repeatedly tried to tell her something until she gave up and out of nowhere said "a stripper, we got Jack a stripper." Obviously, it was a rude thing to say, but for us it is a way of coping with the sometimes soul-destroying reality of Jack's perpetual childlike state. It's not always easy to deal with the fact that Jack isn't able to express himself as a sexual individual and be able to have a girlfriend or get married. As sleazy as it is, I'm sure my parents would be pleased if Jack did have a stripper for his birthday. At least then he'd be behaving like a typical boisterous male. Maybe I'm only guessing here, but I suspect a part of it is true. It's not a subject I like to broach with them or anyone for that matter. Autism and sex is a taboo topic that is routinely swept under the carpet probably out of fear and embarrassment. I can understand that. It is a subject sure to make anyone a little squeamish. How on earth do autistic people, who are by nature dreadful navigators of the social world, initiate a romantic encounter and participate in the highly nuanced verbal and non-verbal language of flirtation?

I've always found it quite strange how sex, something so fundamental to human identity, belonging and biology, is also such a taboo topic. The vast majority of people in this world will seek a sexual partner in this life at some point for company and for reproductive purposes. We are designed to follow these often intense desires for physical as well as emotional affection. Most autistic people are no different in this regard. Most of us at some point in our lives will yearn to satiate our natural biological urges and to keep on doing so over extended periods with a stable romantic partner. I am no different in that respect either, except that my aversion to physical touch and overt displays of physical intimacy prohibit me from doing so. It's an awful conundrum about which I am not really even comfortable speaking to anyone. Not being one to engage in small-talk or be able to read the subtle non-verbal cues so crucial to Western courtship rituals obviously limits my opportunities for romance. If a woman were hinting that she liked me, I most likely would

Birthday cake

not be able to tell. A friend even berated me once for missing an opportunity for a sexual encounter with a woman when we were at the university bar together. The attractive young female who'd invited herself to our table didn't do so just to talk about studying languages as I'd originally thought. Oops!

I was even given the nickname "The Monk" by two friends due to my celibate lifestyle. I wasn't sure how to take it. The seclusion and orderliness of monastic life appeal to my autistic nature, but the lack of sexual activity was obviously a source of amusement to those around me. Several years after university, I'm roughly in the same boat as back then. I did have a relationship of sorts with a girl I met while working as a teacher in China, but it was swiftly terminated by us both. I was not willing to show her affection so could not sustain the relationship because it was, in reality, a platonic intellectual friendship. When it came to sex, I just wasn't ready for it. The idea of being up close and physical with someone else was just too overwhelming for me.

17 – IS HIS AUTISM BETTER YET?

As a family, we're used to people's ignorance when it comes to their understanding of autism. We even appreciate why this is the case and have ceased to berate people for it. The one-sided media portrayals of autism have been pretty lacklustre to say the least. Still, there are certain things people say that are so grossly misinformed that we can't help but feel irked sometimes. When an otherwise intelligent friend of ours once asked us, "Is Jack's autism better now?" we couldn't help but grind our teeth collectively and seethe with rage.

Autism is a lifelong condition and disability. It is not an illness or disease that improves over time. Despite the growth in autism awareness over the past decade, there are still many in the world who think it is akin to having the flu or psoriasis. They believe Jack is infected with a toxin that needs removing, that he's possessed by a kind of demon or that he's simply slower than others to develop. The cognitive laziness of many, even some of those close to us is annoying. Although it is true that autistic people do change over their lifetimes, much in the same way as neurotypical people do, autism is not something that simply "gets better" or "goes away".

It is a condition for life and those who have it are

forced to make the best of it. For many this means embracing a kind of autistic identity and learning to be proud of autism as an essential difference in human neurology rather than a pathological disorder. Such an approach is undeniably more humane than one that insists on trying to fix an autistic individual. However, the attempt to frame autism as a benign difference often trivialises the real suffering many autistic people, particularly those that are severely disabled, face in their daily lives.

Neither Jack nor I can be fixed by any form of trendy new therapy or diet fad. Whatever our circumstance at any given period, our unique individual challenges remain. These challenges may become lesser or greater, but they require constant management. Jack's unvarying routine places a structure on his life that manages his autism better than any therapy or magic formula ever could, while in my case, I've realised just how useful it is to plan for the future and how having a goal in mind can orientate oneself into a positive direction in life. The scientific literature all indicates that those who schedule their lives with future goals in mind enjoy better and more stable emotional health.

After I arrived home from a two-year teaching stint in the

Far East last year, my mind really was in fragments and I knew I needed help. Part of the reason I had been suffering was that I'd been acting in a way that was not in accordance with my autistic nature. I'd denied autism was ever a part of me, considering it to be some kind of nasty pathogen that I could suppress by straining to be like the more socially successful extroverts around me. Lying to others is one thing but lying to oneself for extended periods of time ensnares you in an insidious and hard-to-demolish web of pain and misery. This caused me to have not one but three major depressive breakdowns in my life. It was only upon accepting a label that I'd up until that point dismissed as stigmatising, that my plans for a better life began to fall into place and that I could begin the real task of mapping out the path to a genuinely happy life. Doing so I knew would require effort and planning. It began with small, incremental steps. I had to lose weight and get myself into better shape, so I incorporated a 20-minute walk into my schedule. Added to that were 15 bicep curls. I also wanted to make progress on my book which had been sitting in a dusty corner neglected for months so I made 30 minutes a day for that. Over time, I began to see glimmers of improvement as I became more conditioned to my new, more active routine which was neither too rigid nor too slack. As the neural networks strengthened, the more minutes I was able to do during my walks and the more stamina I had for book writing without resorting to procrastination. In addition to these new routines, I even wrote down a list of what it is I want from life and what I must do to get them. This is something I still glance over regularly to help me stay motivated and to realise why I persist. Here it is:

What can I do to improve myself?

- Lose weight

- Smarten myself up

- Eat less and more frequently

- Get a job

- Establish a more active routine

- Keep my room clean and tidy

- Be nicer to those around me

- Meditate daily

- Buy a games console for relaxation

- Save more money

What would I like for the future?

- To be a healthy weight

- To be less fatigued

- To be able to have my depression under control

- To be able to make money from my writing

- To treat my acid reflux

- To make my parents proud of me once again

- To give money to my grandmother regularly

- To have a pet

- To move into a place of my own

- To find I stable romantic partner I can trust

How can I achieve my goals?

- Through small incremental changes

- By being consistent

- Through hard work

- By being stoical

- By being honest

The voluntary adoption of responsibility is what gives life its meaning. Without the desire to improve oneself to ultimately take on the responsibilities necessary to lead a noble existence, you easily fall prey to nihilism, bitterness and depression. I see this a lot in people like me with Asperger's. Not fitting in with mainstream society often depletes our self-esteem which in turn leads to resentment

A BOOK

and a bad attitude to society in general. Many of us hide away in our rooms, choosing to lose ourselves in video-game fantasies where our inadequacy remains hidden and the grim reality of life outside is at a safe distance. Eventually, this shirking of responsibility catches up with us in hellish ways. We become depressed precisely because of a lack of direction in our lives. We become dependent financially on family members who in turn begin to resent us. Some of us become overweight, even obese due to our lack of physical activity and a lack of motivation to look presentable. I ballooned to 19-stone when I lived on a diet of fast food locked away in my room for almost a year at university. Being in such a state can be fun for a few days, but remain in it for months on end and it becomes intolerable. It kills you and those closest to you physically and spiritually. It is no way to be in the world.

My Asperger's will never improve but what continues to get stronger is my resolve and willingness to find creative ways of being who I am in the world. My unorthodox style often puts me at odds with many around me but by persevering through the chaos and by setting real, achievable goals in my life, I can deal with it. Incessantly whining about unfair things never got anyone anywhere, so instead I attempt in my own unconventional and often bumbling way to make the best of things whilst grabbing onto those rare but wonderful snippets of joy that come about every so often. Onwards and upwards as they say.

18 – AUTISTIC LOVE OF TRAINS

It was at the age of about 16 that my parents first allowed me to take Jack out for the day to provide them a few hours respite. It was during the summer months and the fields a few hundred yards from our house were calling out to be explored and trampled over. Back then we lived as a family in the small commuter town of Epping, a place known to many for being the final stop on London's Central Line. Despite being criss-crossed by motorways and a Tube line, Epping retains a rural feel. My earliest memories were of running through fields of bright yellow rape opposite our first house. These fields were adjacent to the intersection of the M25 and the M11. Amid the ceaseless drone of traffic, I would pick blackberries from the thorny bushes growing next to a big ugly pedestrian footbridge. The whooshing of fast-moving cars was punctuated every few minutes by the clickety-clack and whirring sound of trains that passed underneath the London Orbital.

Trains were the stuff of dreams for me. I'm not sure what it is about them that appealed to me so much at that age, but I suspect it was their benign and unthreatening nature. They are predictable objects which move without deviating from their given path. They're fundamentally honest machines which function in a straightforward manner devoid of the abstract. While many autistic kids are besotted by the inner-workings of trains, my fascination with them ran in a slightly different direction. I paid close attention to the people in the carriages and tried to imagine where their final destination might have been, what job they might have been going to and where they might go to eat at lunchtime. Perhaps they'd opt for a sandwich from Pret-a-Manger and sit by the embankment, watching as throngs of Japanese and American tourists marvel at our heritage. For Jack though, it was all about the trains themselves. He's loved Thomas the Tank Engine since we can all remember and so the chance to retrace our old childhood walks which so fuelled our imaginations, albeit in different ways, was thrilling to us both.

After slapping on some sun cream, we set out with our backpacks. Mum made us both our favourite Marmite sandwiches for the journey. We headed straight for the fields with the aim of reaching the neighbouring village, Theydon Bois, about 2 or 3 miles south of Epping. It was also the next stop on the Central Line. We paraded proudly like two little adventurers, momentarily taking sips from our water bottles as we marched purposely towards the big fields close to our house. The rape fields

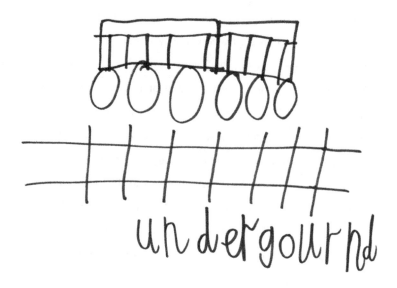

un dergourhd

were now filled with wheat that waved gracefully in the gentle summer breeze.

Before long, we'd reached a hard-baked mud path that scythed through a vast sea of wheat. The distinctive smell of straw was redolent of childhood and took me immediately back to when I was happiest. I remember walking through these same fields when Jack was tiny and my grandmother would hold his hand. Back then, he would carry his favourite cotton blanket everywhere with him. He'd also never leave home without his beloved Fat Controller toy. Even then his love of all things Thomas and tank engines was cemented. Now we were both much more grown up and Jack had finally let go of both of his two favourite things, we were united by both our brotherly bond and a mutual love of railways and, not long after we'd started walking, we could hear the faint whir of a Tube train in the distance. We watched as a line of red and white carriages reflecting the bright summer sunlight sped across the fields, under the motorway and into the distance. It's strange how something so mundane could bring so much pleasure to two brothers. It felt profound, almost dreamlike. As soon as the train was out of earshot, the eerie drone of traffic returned and we carried on walking. As I'd done as a child, I picked and ate a generous handful of blackberries. All these years later, I was most likely eating the descendants of the ones I'd eaten a decade earlier. Some were sweet and delicious and some were tart and unpalatable. I offered Jack a few, but he of course refused. Even a day as special as this wasn't enough to tempt him to try something new. Instead, he took out a banana from his rucksack and munched on it as we crossed that big, ugly old concrete pedestrian bridge over the railway. It was still covered in the same graffiti as years previously and had above it a metal cage to stop people jumping into the path of an oncoming train. Just as we did as children, we stood and gazed at trains both London and Epping-bound, for the best part of an hour. Away from the suspicious gaze of the general public, Jack was able to flap his arms with excitement freely and recite scripts from his favourite Thomas episodes to his heart's content.

After indulging in trains and copious Marmite sandwiches, we carried on walking in the blazing sun through more wheat fields and a grassy meadow peppered with a few cows grazing here and there. At the top of the hill, we looked out at a stunning panoramic view of London. Even from 17 miles away, the capital's centre gleamed and we were able to make out most major landmarks including the NatWest Tower, the then recently constructed Gherkin and Canary Wharf to the East. We both sat in the tranquility of this cool, breezy meadow under a shady oak tree as birds twittered away staring into the vast urban wilderness before us. Both of us were left awestruck by such an incredible view.

Feeling slightly elated, as though we'd discovered a hidden treasure no other had found before, we raced each other down the grassy hill. As we ran, we made revving noises, pretending to be racing cars as we used to do as kids. We both collapsed in a fit of the giggles as we reached the bottom. Such playfulness offered a temporary escape from being our usual selves, defined by unvarying routines and habits. It all felt strangely normal somehow. After walking past a brook into which we both playfully lobbed sticks and stones, we reached the sleepy village of Theydon Bois. This was the first time we'd walked so far without our parents. It was liberating for both of us and exciting, too, so much so that I spontaneously decided to go into a newsagent and buy us both strawberry Cornettos to celebrate. We sat on the village green together, devouring our ice-creams feeling pretty chuffed with ourselves. That was until it dawned on us that we'd have to walk all the way back! By that time, our legs were tired and the sun was scorching. The prospect of traipsing back through the countryside again was not something we relished. That was until we heard the familiar whir of the Tube train in the distance and both of us looked at each other. We'd hop on the train back to Epping to complete our journey. It was a fitting end to an exceptional day as autistic brothers.

It's easy to speak in simple platitudes about autistic people, but more often than not it's better to let them speak for themselves. To understand autism, one must spend long periods in their company, observe them and get to know them. As with everything, the picture you get is far more nuanced than anything you can read in a book or a government-approved pamphlet. Like neurotypicals, autistic people have multi-layered identities, complex personalities and come from diverse cultural backgrounds. They are far from the one-dimensional creatures of popular film renditions and sensationalist literature.

Aside from autistic people themselves, the true holders of knowledge about the condition are the family members, the carers and those who spend days, weeks, months, years and decades working and living alongside them. These people have a level of expertise that goes well beyond that of cold, calculated studies written in science and medical journals. They have a warmer, more intuitive and essentially human rapport with people they don't view as pathological, but as individuals with hopes, dreams, joys and frustrations just like the rest of us. People like this know and accept the challenges involved in caring for an autistic person. They make accommodations for them in ways that allow them to carry on in the way that is at one with their atypical nature.

One such person is Jodie, a full-time employee at Jack's college whom I first got to know when we were colleagues at a local supermarket. She is a special sort of human being who lives to help others and bring joy to those whom society tends to ignore. Her compassionate nature is ideally suited to where she works. Indeed, such compassion is necessary to survive in a job which, due to the complex nature of autism and other neurological conditions, presents challenges beyond what most are used to facing in their daily lives.

Some of the students and residents at St. Elizabeth's are both mentally and physically disabled and some have epilepsy. Many require full-time assistance to carry out the most basic of tasks. Working with such vulnerable people is an angel like Jodie who carries out her work dutifully and with a big smile on her face. It can't be easy cleaning up somebody's mess and having to placate those with challenging behaviours, but she does it because it brings her joy. It's the sort of job that requires a level of dedication and selflessness well beyond the norm.

What is most special about such carers is that they are able to see beyond the disability and get to know the individual. They soon discover that behind the hand flapping, the strange noises and repetitive behaviours is a human being with a unique temperament. When Jodie contacted me to tell me she was working with Jack and that she considered it a real pleasure to do so, I was touched beyond words. Having been conditioned to do all in my power to conceal Jack's disability and to be ashamed of his obviously autistic behaviours, it was consoling to hear someone I know to be totally sincere to say such nice things about my dear little brother. Usually, those who do say nice things come across as quite phony and patronising, but, through working alongside Jack and getting to know him personally, Jodie, like us, was able to delve a little deeper and understand that, much like everyone else, Jack is a person and not just a disability. She described how she got to know him at 'Pets Corner', a part of the college where the students get to interact with and care for a range of animals. Jodie told me how enthusiastically Jack feeds the rabbits with sticks of carrot and celery. It was a heartening thing for me to hear, given how indifferent I thought Jack was towards animals before. She also described how intrigued she was by what she could hear Jack was saying to himself. It all sounded interesting, but of course she had no idea what it all meant! After I explained to her that he does the autistic thing of reciting large chunks of dialogue to himself, she was clearly thrilled. When one understands the reason why, one develops a much fuller picture. Autism can often seem mysterious to an outsider, but with a little perseverance and time spent in the company of those on the spectrum, it begins to make a bit more sense.

Another discovery we as a family made during our time networking with other autistic families from across the UK is just how different autistic people are. This shouldn't really have been much of a surprise of course, but like a lot of people, we all believed that autism was a uniform condition. Instead, we met autistic people with various personalities and temperaments. Some were pleasant and agreeable, some were less nice. Some were gregarious and chatty, and some were painfully shy and introverted. Some were adventurous in their eating habits, and some were severely limited. What we discovered was that the label of autism should not define the individual. As the popular saying goes, "If you've met one person with autism, you've met one person with autism."

It's for this reason that I fundamentally trust people like Jodie, who work with a broad range of autistic people each day, more than I do any clinician or any self-appointed spokesperson for the autism community. Whereas the clinical expert sees patterns of behaviours, rabbit and chicken

sets of emotional responses and activity in the brain, a carer like Jodie sees a human being and forms with that human being a bond built on a solid foundation of love and empathy. Such an intimate one-to-one connection is not something that can be quantified, peer-reviewed and backed up by double-blind studies. It has to be felt and it is that level of feeling for autistic people that I want to encourage. Science may help us to conceptualise and frame the condition, but the lived experiences of autistic people and those of the family members and carers who are close to them, convey the true soul of autism.

20 – THE FUTURE

I don't like thinking about the future but as my parents grow older and the time when they will no longer be able to look after Jack gets nearer, planning ahead becomes a necessity. I am reluctant to ask them questions about what happens next out of a deep and terrifying fear that it might open up the sluice gates. When I see my family, I avoid any such discussion and prefer to live in the present moment, grasping at what joy there is to be had while it lasts. It's usually at an ungodly hour like 3am that my most troubling thoughts come to the surface.

There are so many questions I simply don't know the answers to, like what happens when mum and dad leave this world and it's just Jack and me? Will he live with me or go into full-time care? Will I even have my own life together into some semblance of functional normality by then? Am I responsible enough to even assume the responsibility of being Jack's carer and legal guardian? Will I even be alive myself by then? My chronic tiredness and proneness to bouts of severe depression are hardly good indicators of a long and fruitful life. Time feels as though it's constantly running out. As I approach 30 I fear I'm not advancing fast enough into a state fit enough to be someone my family can rely on. Hitherto, I have not picked up a heavy enough load and carried it with me.

I've been feckless, disorientated and nihilistic in my outlook. I have my problems as a man on the autism spectrum. Asperger's is above all a social disability and being unable to connect in a meaningful sense to those around me has made me weak in almost every facet of my life. Human beings, for better or for worse, are social animals. We're team players who rely on one another for support, guidance and survival. For me to carry on as a perpetual loner as I often have done would be a disadvantage not only to myself but also to my entire family. There has come a point in my life when I see the necessity of being more conventional, of building bridges, of bonding with others and of being a more social human being.

It is necessary to have others on whom you can depend to support you. It is vital for one's survival in a reality that can easily fragment, disintegrate and descend into unbearable chaos. That chaos will arise unless I strengthen myself and my ties into the outside world. When my parents leave this world, I can't afford for Jack's sake to dissolve into a useless mess. I have to be strong.

In a typically autistic fashion, I've made a concerted effort to maintain friendships by drawing up lists of people to contact and schedules of when I should get in contact with them next. My Aspergian personality is not naturally inclined to be sociable and considerate of the social needs of others. Like I have done in many other instances, I now impose my own structure on the things that are chaotic and abstract in my mind. My aim is to reinforce this habit in the hope that it may become a part of me and that, when the fated day comes when it's Jack and me, I won't necessarily be alone. I'll have someone or perhaps many others who can comfort me and be able to look at the situation with dispassion and freshness, enabling me to find solutions to the inevitable problems that will arise. That is my hope.

I am a keen admirer of the Buddha but it wasn't until events started to happen in my own life that I understood the fundamental Buddhist dictum "Life is suffering". Life is indeed hard, often tragic and full of the most deplorable suffering. The Buddha, who grew up in luxurious opulence, chose voluntarily to face the suffering outside his palace walls rather than sheltering himself from it and in that way was able to transcend it. He came up with the revolutionary notion that few of us grasp or even admit, namely, that suffering is caused not so much by external forces but by our own internal reaction to those inevitable factors of existence. Buddha imposed his own method and structure to deal with this without descending into nihilism. The method or 'dharma' transcends suffering by recognising its causes and facing up to it squarely and bravely. It requires one to stake one's life on the bitter truths of one's existence and in that way it frees you from bitterness.

You could say I've come up with my own autistic method or 'dharma' in dealing with the difficulties and inevitable suffering involved in being disabled myself and having a profoundly disabled brother. By working in such a manner, I have reduced my own anxieties about what happens next because I know that, when the times comes, I might just be strong enough to deal with things rationally and calmly. I'll be someone, imperfect, impetuous and imbecilic as I often am, who nonetheless did his best to be strong, dependable and loving. Telling my story is a key part of that process of transformation. Humans live in stories and speak of their own lives as ongoing and ever-changing narratives replete with twists, turns and complications. We can plan as best as we can for the future but we never can predict quite what's next around the corner. The best we can do is become the best person we can be whilst accepting the fact of our own appalling vulnerability. Turning my own life around for the sake of Jack and my family has been predicated entirely on being entirely straight with myself and others. Now that's hard sometimes. If we're totally honest with ourselves, we're often not that honest with ourselves. We omit things we don't like, we do our best to conceal inconvenient truths that threaten the structures of our own delusions and fantasies, and we wear a mask before others in the hope we gain their approval. Such dishonesty prolongs our suffering and, as I write this final chapter, I grow more convinced that it is through the power of honest communication that one's ideas are the best chance anyone has of resolving the continually emergent problems we face in our lives.

My brother Jack is an embodiment of pure innocence. Ever since that day mum brought him home and I, as a little toddler, dabbed polo mints on his lips, I've had a deep desire to protect him. As I grow older, I realise that the most meaningful thing I can do for him is to shore myself up, to be consistent, to stake my life on being a responsible elder brother. Life may not be ideal, it may often be unfair for us, but incessantly complaining is not a noble way to be in the face of it. To get the most out of it one has to face it bravely and part of that is not wearing a permanent grimace. Being brave necessitates having a smile on one's face and being joyful in the face of sadness. Through the challenges, both Jack and I will both be smiling together. Between autistic brothers, no rivalry is necessary. We are a team.

the
end

Made in the USA
Middletown, DE
14 March 2020